WAYS OF STAYING STEADFAST UPON THE RELIGION

Shaykh Abdur-Razzaq Ibn Abdil-Muhsin al-Badr

ISBN: 978-1-9442-4519-1
First Edition: Safar 1437 A.H./November 2015 C.E.
Cover Design: Abu Sulaymaan Muhammad AbdulAzim bin Joshua Baker

Translation by: Muhammad ibn Adnan Abu Harb
Revision & Editing by: Maktabatulirshad staff
Typesetting & Formatting by: Aboo Sulaymaan Muhammad 'AbdulAzim

Printing: Ohio Printing
Subject: Aqeedah
Website: www.maktabatulirshad.com
E-mail: info@maktabatulirshad.com

Table of Contents

BRIEF BIOGRAPHY OF THE AUTHOR

His name: Shaykh 'Abdur-Razzaaq Bin 'AbdilMuhsin Al-'Abbad Al-Badr. He is the son of Al-'Allamah Muhaddith of Medina Shaykh 'Abdul-Muhsin Al-'Abbad Al-Badr.

Birth: He was born on the 22nd day of Dhul-Qaddah in he year 1382 AH in az-Zal'fi, Kingdom of Saudia Arabia. He currently resides in Al-Medina AlMunawwarah.

Current occupation: He is a member of the teaching staff in the Islamic University, in Al-Medina.

Scholastic certifications: Doctorate in 'Aqeedah.

The Shaykh has authored books, researches, as well as numerous explanations in different sciences. Among them:

1. Fiqh of Supplications & Ad-Dhkaar.

2. Hajj & refinement of Souls,

3. Explanation of the book "Exemplary Principles" By Shaykh 'Uthaymeen (May Allah have mercy upon him).

4. Explanation of the book "the principles of Names & Attributes" authored by Shaykh-ul-Islam Ibnul Qayyim (May Allah have mercy upon him).

5. Explanation of the book "Good Words" authored by Shaykh-ul-Islam Ibn Qayyim (May Allah have mercy upon him).

6. Explanation of the book "Aqeedah Tahaawiyyah".

7. Explanation of the book "Fusuul: Biography of the Messenger) By Ibn Katheer (May Allah have mercy upon him).

8. He has a full explanation of the book "Aadaab-ul-Muf'rad" authored by Imam Bukhari (May Allah have mercy upon him).

From the most distinguished scholars whom he has taken knowledge and acquired knowledge from are:

1. His father Al-'Allamah Shaykh 'Abdul-Muhsin AlBadr—may Allah preserve him.

2. Al-'Allamah Shaykh Ibn Baaz—may Allah have mercy upon him.

3. Al-'Allamah Shaykh Muhammad Bin Saleh Al'Uthaymeen—may Allah have mercy upon him.

4. Shaykh 'Ali Nasir Faqeehi—may Allah preserve him.

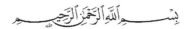

INTRODUCTION

All praise belongs to Allah the Lord of the Worlds. I bear witness that there is no deity that has the right to be worshipped except Allah, He is alone and has no partner; and I bear witness that Muhammad is His servant and His Messenger. May Allah raise his status and bestow peace upon him, his family, and all of his companions. O Allah, teach us that which will benefit us, and benefit us with that which you have taught us; and increase us in beneficial knowledge. (O Allah) rectify for us all of our affair, and do not leave us to ourselves for the blinking of an eye.

To precede:

Noble gathering, congratulations to you for this gathering in a house from the houses of Allah (Blessed and Exalted is He). (This gathering) is not for anything else except to study the religion of Allah (Blessed and Exalted is He) and to increase in the provision of faith. Our noble Prophet (May Allah raise his status and bestow upon him peace) said:

مَا اجْتَمَعَ قَوْمٌ فِي بَيْتٍ مِنْ بُيُوتِ اللهِ يَتْلُونَ كِتَابَ اللهِ وَيَتَدَارَسُونَهُ بَيْنَهُمْ إِلَّا نَزَلَتْ عَلَيْهِمِ السَّكِينَةُ، وَغَشِيَتْهُمُ الرَّحْمَةُ، وَحَفَّتْهُمُ الْمَلَائِكَةُ، وَذَكَرَهُمُ اللهُ فِيمَنْ عِنْدَهُ

"A people do not gather in a house from the houses of Allah reciting the book of Allah, and studying it amongst themselves, except that tranquility descends upon them, mercy covers them, the angels encompass them, and Allah mentions them to those who are with Him."

It has been established in Saheeh Muslim from the hadith of Muaawiyah (May Allah be pleased with him) who said:

خَرَجَ رَسُولَ اللهِ صَلَّى اللهُ عَلَيْهِ وَسَلَّمَ عَلَى حَلْقَةٍ مِنْ أَصْحَابِهِ فَقَالَ: ((مَا أَجْلَسَكُمْ؟)) قَالُوا: «جَلَسْنَا نَذْكُرُ اللهَ وَنَحْمَدُهُ عَلَى مَا هَدَانَا لِلْإِسْلَامِ وَمَنَّ بِهِ عَلَيْنَا»، قَالَ عليه الصلاة والسلام: ((آللَّهِ مَا أَجْلَسَكُمْ إِلَّا ذَاكَ؟)) قَالُوا: «وَاللهِ مَا أَجْلَسَنَا إِلَّا ذَاكَ»، قَالَ: ((أَمَا إِنِّي لَمْ أَسْتَحْلِفْكُمْ تُهْمَةً لَكُمْ، وَلَكِنَّهُ أَتَانِي جِبْرِيلُ فَأَخْبَرَنِي أَنَّ اللهَ عَزَّ وَجَلَّ يُبَاهِي بِكُمُ الْمَلَائِكَةَ

"The Messenger of Allah (May Allah raise his status and bestow upon him peace) went out to an assembly of his companions and said:

"What has made you sit here?"

So they said:

> **"We have sat to remember Allah and praise Him for guiding us to Islam, and for what He has bestowed upon us (of favors)."**

The Prophet (May Allah raise his status and bestow upon him peace) said:

> **"By Allah, nothing made you sit except that?"**

The companions said:

> **"By Allah, nothing made us sit except that."**

The Prophet (May Allah raise his status and bestow upon him peace) said:

> **"I did not make you swear (by Allah) to accuse you, but Jibreel came to me and informed me that Allah talks proudly of you to the angels."**

So to Allah belongs the praise firstly and lastly, and to Him belongs thanks openly and secretly. We ask Allah - Exalted in His loftiness- who has made this meeting and gathering easy for us that He allows us to achieve the good, the blessing, the profit, and the benefit. And to make this sitting of ours as a proof for us and not against us, and a benefit for us guiding us to the straight path of Allah (Blessed and Exalted is He). May Allah thank those in charge for this blessed beneficial reward -Allah willing- as well as their efforts, their service, and their organizing of this meeting and gathering, which I ask Allah (Glorified and Exalted) to allow us to achieve in it benefit and good. And that He rewards those in charge for this requital, their praiseworthy efforts, their service in organizing this meeting, and the likes of these beneficial gatherings.

Noble gathering, the talk in this gathering of ours is about "Ways and reasons to stay firm upon the religion". It is no doubt that studying the likes of this subject is very important. The Muslim is in dire need of studying the likes of this every now and then. This is because the ways and the reasons that take a person to the right and to the left, hinder him from good, and turn him away from guidance are of many different types. The calamities that deter (a person) from guidance come from different ways. Therefore, the servant (of Allah) - and this is the situation- is to give tremendous careful diligence to the ways of staying firm upon the truth and guidance. Especially since the heart of the son of Adam is afflicted with affairs, which are from doubts or desires, thus turning him away and deviating him from the straight path of Allah (Blessed and Exalted is He). Rather, it has been established from our noble Prophet (May Allah raise his status and bestow upon him peace) that he said:

لَقَلْبُ ابْنِ آدَمَ أَشَدُّ انْقِلَابًا مِنْ الْقِدْرِ إِذَا اجْتَمَعَتْ غَلْيًا

"The heart of the son of Adam turns more than that of a pot when it boils."

Likewise it has been established from him (May Allah raise his status and bestow upon him peace) that he said:

$$مَثَلُ الْقَلْبِ مَثَلُ رِيشَةٍ بِأَرْضٍ فَلَاةٍ تُقَلِّبُهَا الرِّيَاحُ$$

"The likeness of the heart is the likeness of a feather on the ground of the desert blown around by the wind."

The heart was not called (Qalb) except due to its turning and changing. Due to this most of the supplication of our Prophet (May Allah raise his status and bestow upon him peace) used to be:

$$يَا مُقَلِّبَ القُلُوبِ ثَبِّتْ قَلْبِي عَلَى دِينِكَ$$

"O Changer of hearts keep my heart frim upon your religion."

On the authority of Umm Salama (May Allah be pleased with her) who said:

"Most of the supplication of the Messenger of Allah (May Allah raise his status and bestow upon him peace) used to be:

"O Changer of hearts keep my heart firm upon your religion."

Umm Salama said, so I said: "Do the hearts turn?!" The Prophet (May Allah raise his status and bestow upon him peace) said:

مَا مِنْ قَلْبٍ إِلَّا بَيْنَ إِصْبَعَيْنِ مِنْ أَصَابِعِ الرَّحْمَنِ يُقَلِّبُهَا كَيْفَ يَشَاءُ ؛ إِنْ شَاءَ أَقَامَهُ، وَإِنْ شَاءَ أَزَاغَهُ

"There is no heart except that it is between the two fingers of the fingers of the Most Merciful He turns it as He wills. If He wills He makes it steadfast, and if He wills He causes it to deviate."

We ask Allah the Magnificent that He makes us firm upon the truth and guidance, and that He protects us from deviation, misguidance, destruction, and ruin.

Especially since the restless overwhelming tribulations are very many, which agitate the people, destroy them, and take them here and there deviating (them) from the straight path of Allah (Blessed and Exalted), except the one whom Allah saves, protects, and preserves. And in Saheeh Muslim on the authority of the Prophet (May Allah raise his status and bestow upon him peace) who said:

تُعْرَضُ الْفِتَنُ عَلَى الْقُلُوبِ كَالْحَصِيرِ عُودًا عُودًا، فَأَيُّ قَلْبٍ أُشْرِبَهَا نُكِتَ فِيهِ نُكْتَةٌ سَوْدَاءُ، وَأَيُّ قَلْبٍ أَنْكَرَهَا نُكِتَ فِيهِ نُكْتَةٌ بَيْضَاءُ ، حَتَّى تَصِيرَ عَلَى قَلْبَيْنِ : عَلَى أَبْيَضَ مِثْلِ

الصَّفَا فَلَا تَضُرُّهُ فِتْنَةٌ مَا دَامَتِ السَّمَاوَاتُ وَالْأَرْضُ ، وَالْآخَرُ
-وهو القلب الذي أُشرب الفتنة- أَسْوَدُ مُرْبَادًّا كَالْكُوزِ
مُجَخِّيًا)) بهذا وصفه عليه الصلاة والسلام ((أَسْوَدُ مُرْبَادًّا
كَالْكُوزِ مُجَخِّيًا ، لَا يَعْرِفُ مَعْرُوفًا وَلَا يُنْكِرُ مُنْكَرًا إِلَّا مَا
أُشْرِبَ مِنْ هَوَاهُ)) . نسأل الله العافية

"Trials and tribulations are presented to the heart like that of a straw mat woven stick by stick. So which ever heart is penetrated by them (i.e. the trials and tribulations) will have a black spot put on it. And which every heart rejects it will have a white spot placed on it. Until there becomes two types of hearts: one white like a white stone which will not be harmed by tribulations as long as the heavens and the earth remain. And the other (type of heart) -and it is the heart that is penetrated with tribulation- will be black and blurred like an overturned vessel"

This is what he (May Allah raise his status and bestow upon him peace) described it with being

"Black and blurred like that of an overturned vessel, not knowing good, and not rejecting evil, but rather immersed in its desires."

We ask Allah for wellbeing. This (hadith) clarifies the dangers of tribulations, and that trials are presented to the hearts. Some of the scholars have said regarding the meaning of (trials) are presented to the hearts: That trials and tribulations stick to the hearts, and it will be stuck in the heart that is presented (with these trials), just like that of the straw mat when a person sleeps on it and his body sticks to it; thus a mark from the mat is left on his body due to it being stuck to him.

Likewise this is the affair of tribulations when it comes to the heart. However, the heart of the Muslim rejects (these tribulations), and does not accept them. As for other than that then it is immersed in tribulations; and this means that they penetrate in one's heart and are deeply rooted in him, and Allah's refuge is sought.

TRIBULATIONS ARE OF TWO TYPES

The tribulations that the heart is afflicted with are of two types:

1. Tribulations of doubts
2. Tribulations of desires

As for the tribulation of doubts then it results from corrupt concepts, deficient knowledge, and weak insight. As for tribulations of desires than it emanates from (one having) weak determination, feeble will, low aspiration, and the souls inclination to its lusts and desires without concern for the limits of the legislation, and the regulations of the religion. The tribulations of doubts are corruption in knowledge, and the tribulations of desires is corruption in action. A person will not be upright upon the religion of Allah (Blessed and Exalted) except by him being upright upon beneficial knowledge and righteous action, Allah said:

$$﴿هُوَ الَّذِى أَرْسَلَ رَسُولَهُ بِالْهُدَىٰ وَدِينِ الْحَقِّ لِيُظْهِرَهُ عَلَى الدِّينِ كُلِّهِ﴾$$

"It is He who sent His Messenger with the guidance and the religion of truth so that He may cause it to prevail over all religions." [As-Saff: 9]

Guidance is beneficial knowledge, and the religion of truth is righteous action. The servant will not be upon the truth, guidance, and safety from doubts and desires, except by him adhering to this way and being concern with it; beneficial knowledge and righteous action. Since this status and matter is the loftiest of statuses, and the greatest of matters. Allah (Glorified and Exalted) ordered His servants to adhere to supplicating Him to be guided to the straight path. Rather, He ordered this upon His servants every day and night; seventeen times in the obligatory prayer.

﴿اهْدِنَا الصِّرَاطَ الْمُسْتَقِيمَ ۞ صِرَاطَ الَّذِينَ أَنْعَمْتَ عَلَيْهِمْ غَيْرِ الْمَغْضُوبِ عَلَيْهِمْ وَلَا الضَّالِّينَ ۞﴾

"Guide us to the straight path" "The path of those whom You have bestowed Your grace. Not (the way of) those who earned Your anger nor those who went astray." [Al-Faatihah 6-7]

- Those whom Allah has bestowed His grace are those whom Allah has combined for them between beneficial knowledge and righteous action.

- Those whom have earned Allah's wrath are those who have knowledge but don't act upon it, as Allah said about the Jews:

$$﴿مَثَلُ الَّذِينَ حُمِّلُوا التَّوْرَاةَ ثُمَّ لَمْ يَحْمِلُوهَا كَمَثَلِ الْحِمَارِ يَحْمِلُ أَسْفَارًا﴾$$

"The likeness of those who were entrusted with the torah, but failed to implement it is like the donkey that carries huge books." [Al-Jumu'ah:5]

"They did not implement it", meaning they did not act upon it.

- The one who is misguided is he who does a deed and is diligent in acts of worship but has no knowledge nor insight in the religion of Allah (Blessed and Exalted)

Therefore, safety and benefit will only (take place) by actualizing these two affairs together; beneficial knowledge and righteous action. So with beneficial knowledge a person will be saved by Allah permission from overwhelming doubts. And with righteous action and uprightness upon it, a person will be saved by Allah's permission from destructive desires.

It must be known – noble gathering- that the affair of being steadfast upon the truth and guidance is in the hand of Allah (Glorified and Exalted). And He (Glorified and Exalted) is the One whom the hearts of the servants are in His hand. They (i.e. His servants) are subject to His disposal and His subjection. Whatever Allah wills will be and what every He does not will, will never be, and there is no power nor might except with Allah. To Allah belongs the affair from before and after, and all of the affairs of the servants are in His hand

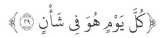

"Every day He is (engaged) in an affair."
[Ar-Rahman 29]

(Allah) guides and misguides, honors and disgraces, abases and raises, gives and prevents, withholds (the provision) and enlarges (the provision), He makes (people laugh) and cry, He gives life and death. The affair is His affair, and all of the creation are subject to His disposal (Glorified and Exalted). Being steadfast is in the hand of Allah. It is He who gives success, aides and guides to the straight path. Allah (Blessed and Exalted is He) said:

﴿ يُثَبِّتُ اللَّهُ الَّذِينَ آمَنُوا بِالْقَوْلِ الثَّابِتِ فِي الْحَيَاةِ الدُّنْيَا وَفِي الْآخِرَةِ ۖ وَيُضِلُّ اللَّهُ الظَّالِمِينَ ۚ وَيَفْعَلُ اللَّهُ مَا يَشَاءُ ۝ ﴾

"Allah makes firm those who believe with the statement of firmness in the life of this   world,

and Allah misguides the wrongdoers. And Allah does what He wills." [Ibrahim 27]

If the Muslim knows this tremendous foundation in this matter – and it is that steadfastness is an affair that is in the hand of Allah- then the servant is to give great importance to turning to Allah, having good reliance upon Him, and putting complete trust in Him (Glorified and Exalted); (while) hoping from Him alone that Allah makes him firm, guides him, rectifies his heart, and protects him from deviation, and misguidance. Thus, the affair is His affair (Glorified and Exalted). Due to this there are many supplications that have been reported in achieving this affair, and in attaining this firmness. And from that is what has come in the noble Quran:

$$﴿رَبَّنَا لَا تُزِغْ قُلُوبَنَا بَعْدَ إِذْ هَدَيْتَنَا وَهَبْ لَنَا مِن لَّدُنكَ رَحْمَةً ۚ إِنَّكَ أَنتَ الْوَهَّابُ ٨ ﴾$$

"Our Lord do not deviate our hearts after you have guided us, and grant us mercy from You, indeed You are the One who bestows" [Ali Imran 8]

Also there are many (supplications) from our noble Prophet (May Allah raise his status and bestow upon him peace) dealing with this matter, and from them is the supplication that has preceded, which used to be most of the supplication of our Prophet (May Allah raise his status and bestow upon him peace) "O Changer of hearts keep my heart firm upon your religion." It comes in al-Bukhari and Muslim that our noble Prophet (May Allah raise his status and bestow upon him peace) said in his supplication:

اللهُمَّ لَكَ أَسْلَمْتُ، وَبِكَ آمَنْتُ، وَعَلَيْكَ تَوَكَّلْتُ، وَإِلَيْكَ أَنَبْتُ، وَبِكَ خَاصَمْتُ، اللهُمَّ إِنِّي أَعُوذُ بِعِزَّتِكَ لَا إِلَهَ إِلَّا أَنْتَ أَنْ تُضِلَّنِي، أَنْتَ الْحَيُّ الَّذِي لَا يَمُوتُ، وَالْجِنُّ وَالْإِنْسُ يَمُوتُونَ

"O Allah, to you I submit, in You I believe, in You I put my trust, to You I will return, and for you I dispute. O Allah, I seek refuge in Your honor- there is no god who has the right to be worshipped but You- that You misguide me. You are the Ever-Living who never dies; but jinn and mankind will (all) die."

Also it has come from the Prophet (May Allah raise his status and bestow upon him peace) that he called upon the one who left his home for any benefit from the benefits of the religion or the worldly life that they say:

اللَّهُمَّ أَعُوذُ بِكَ أَنْ أَضِلَّ أَوْ أُضَلَّ، أَوْ أَزِلَّ أَوْ أُزَلَّ، أَوْ أَظْلِمَ أَوْ أُظْلَمَ، أَوْ أَجْهَلَ أَوْ يُجْهَلَ عَلَيَّ

"O Allah, I seek refuge in You that I stray or become misguided, that I fall into error or that I'm made to fall into error, that I oppress (others) or that I'm oppressed, or that I am

ignorant or that I'm treated in an ignorant manner."

Also from the reported supplications from the Prophet (May Allah raise his status and bestow upon him peace) in this affair is the hadith of Ali (May Allah be pleased with him) when he requested from the Prophet (May Allah raise his status and bestow upon him peace) that he teach him a supplication that he could supplicate to Allah with it. He (May Allah raise his status and bestow upon him peace) said:

$$قُلِ اللهُمَّ اهْدِنِي وَسَدِّدْنِي، وَاذْكُرْ بِالْهُدَى هِدَايَتَكَ الطَّرِيقَ، وَالسَّدَادِ سَدَادَ السَّهْمِ$$

"Say, O Allah, guide me and set me aright", and remember (when you ask Allah) to guide you then think of the straight path, and when you ask Him to set you aright (remember) the aiming of the arrow."

And the supplications with this meaning are many.

So with this it becomes known –noble gathering- that from the greatest ways of staying steadfast, and the most important of (these ways) is supplicating, turning to Allah for help by requesting that (from Him), while putting great trust in Allah, having strong reliance upon Him, having complete recourse to Him, asking Him for firmness, and seeking refuge (in Him) from deviation and misguidance. And Allah does not disappoint the one who calls upon Him, nor does He turndown the one who calls out to Him –and He (Glorified and Exalted is the One) who said:

$$﴿وَإِذَا سَأَلَكَ عِبَادِى عَنِّى فَإِنِّى قَرِيبٌ ۖ أُجِيبُ دَعْوَةَ الدَّاعِ إِذَا دَعَانِ ۖ فَلْيَسْتَجِيبُوا لِى وَلْيُؤْمِنُوا بِى لَعَلَّهُمْ يَرْشُدُونَ ١٨٦﴾$$

"And if My servants ask about Me then I am near. I respond to the supplication of the one who calls Me. So let them obey Me and believe in Me so that they may be guided to the right path." [Al-Baqarah 186]

Likewise Allah said:

$$﴿وَقَالَ رَبُّكُمُ ادْعُونِى أَسْتَجِبْ لَكُمْ ۚ إِنَّ الَّذِينَ يَسْتَكْبِرُونَ عَنْ عِبَادَتِى سَيَدْخُلُونَ جَهَنَّمَ دَاخِرِينَ ٦٠﴾$$

"And your Lord said," Call upon Me and I will respond to you. Indeed, those who turn away from My worship will enter the hell fire in humiliation." [Ghafir 60]

So we ask Allah by His beautiful names and His lofty attributes- and because He is Allah whom none has the right to be worshipped but Him, and because He

(Glorified and Exalted) is the changer and the turner of the hearts- that He makes all of us firm upon the truth and guidance, and that He protects us all from deviation and misguidance. Indeed, He (Blessed and Exalted) is the All- Hearer, near (to His servants thru His knowledge), and responds (to the supplication of His servants who call upon Him alone).

GIVING GREAT CONCERN TO THE NOBLE QURAN

And from the greatest ways of staying steadfast upon the truth and guidance is giving great concern to the noble Quran; the book of guidance, the book of steadfastness and uprightness. Allah (Blessed and Exalted) said:

﴿إِنَّ هَٰذَا الْقُرْآنَ يَهْدِى لِلَّتِي هِيَ أَقْوَمُ وَيُبَشِّرُ الْمُؤْمِنِينَ الَّذِينَ يَعْمَلُونَ الصَّالِحَاتِ أَنَّ لَهُمْ أَجْرًا كَبِيرًا ۝﴾

"Verily, this Quran guides to that which is most just, and it gives glad tidings to the believers who do righteous deeds, that they will have a tremendous reward." [Al-Isra 9]

Therefore, giving great concern to this tremendous book by reading it, contemplating the Quran's meanings and what they indicate; as well as striving against (one's) soul in acting its advises and its guidance is from the affairs that assists (an individual) upon steadfastness. Allah (Glorified and Exalted) said:

﴿وَقَالَ الَّذِينَ كَفَرُوا لَوْلَا نُزِّلَ عَلَيْهِ الْقُرْآنُ جُمْلَةً وَاحِدَةً ۚ كَذَٰلِكَ لِنُثَبِّتَ بِهِ فُؤَادَكَ ۖ وَرَتَّلْنَاهُ تَرْتِيلًا ۝﴾

"Those who disbelieved said," If only the Quran was revealed to him at once." Thus, that We make your heart firm with it. And We have revealed it in stages." [Al-Furqan 32]

So that which is benefited from this verse is that the Muslims concern for reciting the Quran, reflecting upon the Quran's meanings, and the guidance of the Quran; and thereafter striving against (ones) soul by acting upon it, is from the greatest causes and reasons for steadfastness. Allah (Glorified and Exalted) said:

$$﴿ وَإِذَا مَا أُنزِلَتْ سُورَةٌ فَمِنْهُم مَّن يَقُولُ أَيُّكُمْ$$
$$زَادَتْهُ هَٰذِهِ إِيمَانًا ۚ فَأَمَّا الَّذِينَ آمَنُوا فَزَادَتْهُمْ$$
$$إِيمَانًا وَهُمْ يَسْتَبْشِرُونَ ۝ ﴾$$

"When a surah is revealed, from them are those who say," Which of you has had this (surah) increase him in faith?" As for those who believe it increases them in faith, and they rejoice." [At-Tawbah 124]

This is the affair of the Quran with those who give concern to it; those who reflect upon its verses, those who contemplate its meanings, as well as what they indicate. And due to this there are verses in the Quran encouraging the contemplation of the book of Allah.

Allah said:

﴿أَفَلَا يَتَدَبَّرُونَ الْقُرْآنَ أَمْ عَلَى قُلُوبٍ أَقْفَالُهَا ٢٤﴾

"Do they not reflect about the Quran? Or are there locks upon their hearts?!)** [Muhammad 24]

And Allah said:

﴿أَفَلَا يَتَدَبَّرُونَ الْقُرْآنَ وَلَوْ كَانَ مِنْ عِندِ غَيْرِ اللَّهِ لَوَجَدُوا فِيهِ اخْتِلَافًا كَثِيرًا ٨٢﴾

"Do they not ponder over the Quran? Had it been from other than Allah they would certainly found much contradiction in it." [An-Nisaa 82]

Likewise Allah said:

﴿كِتَابٌ أَنزَلْنَاهُ إِلَيْكَ مُبَارَكٌ لِيَدَّبَّرُوا آيَاتِهِ وَلِيَتَذَكَّرَ أُولُو الْأَلْبَابِ ٢٩﴾

"A book that We have revealed to you, filled with blessings, so that they may reflect upon its verses, and so that men of understanding may remember." [Saad 29]

Rather, Allah has informed in the noble Quran, that this Quran, and a person's concern for reflecting upon it, is from the greatest causes for being saved from misguidance, turning back on one's heels, and deviating from the straight path. So ponder over this meaning in the statement of Allah (Glorified and Exalted):

﴿قَدْ كَانَتْ آيَاتِي تُتْلَىٰ عَلَيْكُمْ فَكُنتُمْ عَلَىٰ أَعْقَابِكُمْ تَنكِصُونَ ۝ مُسْتَكْبِرِينَ بِهِ سَامِرًا تَهْجُرُونَ ۝ أَفَلَمْ يَدَّبَّرُوا الْقَوْلَ﴾

"My verses used to be recited to you, however you turned back on your heels. In pride speaking badly about it (i.e. the Quran) at night. Have they not pondered upon the word...?" [Al-Muminoon 66-68]

Meaning that had they reflected upon the word (i.e. the Quran), and gave concern to pondering over the guidance of the noble Quran, then that would have been a cause for their safety from turning back on (their) heels. Thus, in the Quran is a protection from falsehood and a safety from deviation and misguidance. Due to this Allah (Glorified and Exalted) said:

﴿وَاعْتَصِمُوا بِحَبْلِ اللَّهِ جَمِيعًا وَلَا تَفَرَّقُوا﴾

"Hold firm to the rope of Allah and be not divide amongst yourselves." [Ali Imran 103]

And due to this it is imperative upon the Muslim-especially with the many trials, their types, and their severity upon a person when it comes to the two affairs of doubts and desires- that he makes for himself a portion from the book of Allah; reading it, reflecting upon it, pondering upon the noble Quran's meanings, and striving against (ones) soul to act by it, in order to actualize the statement of Allah (Glorified and Exalted):

$$﴿الَّذِينَ آتَيْنَاهُمُ الْكِتَابَ يَتْلُونَهُ حَقَّ تِلَاوَتِهِ أُولَٰئِكَ يُؤْمِنُونَ بِهِ﴾$$

"Those whom We gave the book they recite it the way that it should be recited, they are those who believe in it. [Al-Baqarah 121]

May Allah make us all from them by His favor and His honor.

BEING CONCERNED WITH PERFORMING GOOD DEEDS

Noble gathering, also from the ways of staying frim upon the religion is being concerned with performing good deeds, seeking nearness to Allah, and striving against one's soul in that. Indeed, the soul is free and liberated, therefore it is in need of the servant to strive against itself; persistent upon the truth, guidance, and diligence upon that. As Allah (Blessed and Exalted) said:

$$﴿وَالَّذِينَ جَاهَدُوا فِينَا لَنَهْدِيَنَّهُمْ سُبُلَنَا ۚ وَإِنَّ اللَّهَ لَمَعَ الْمُحْسِنِينَ ۝﴾$$

"Those who strive for Us, then We shall certainly guide them to Our ways. Verily, Allah is with the good-doers." [Al-Ankaboot 69]

So fighting against ones soul in performing good deeds, acts of worship, and seeking nearness to Allah is from the reasons for having great firmness (upon the religion). Ponder upon this meaning in the noble verse (where) Allah said:

﴿ يُثَبِّتُ اللَّهُ الَّذِينَ آمَنُوا بِالْقَوْلِ الثَّابِتِ فِى
الْحَيَاةِ الدُّنْيَا وَفِى الْآخِرَةِ ﴾

"Allah makes firm those who believe with the statement of firmness in the life of this world and the hereafter." [Ibrahim 27]

Verily, faith and being concern about it is a cause for a person steadfastness; and that is the believing servant considers his faith the most precious and valuable thing that he owns. And that his adherence to his faith, and his observance of his religion is greater than that of the people of this world for their worldly life. Also he takes account of himself when it comes to the affairs of the religion and his deeds, even more so than the accounting of those who have money as it relates to the affair of gaining and earning wealth, and being safe from losing profit. Indeed, the believer considers his faith and his religion the most precious thing that he owns and the most valuable thing that he possesses. His concern for his region is of great concern in belief and action.

If this was his perseverance, observance, and concern for his religion, then that is a reason–by Allah's permission – for Allah making him firm upon the truth and guidance. And because of this, the soundness of belief, and the striving of the soul upon upright action is a reason for steadfastness. At this point we reflect upon that which has been reported from the Prophet (May Allah raise his

status and bestow upon him peace) in the authentic
hadith where he said:

إِنَّ الرَّجُلَ لَيَعْمَلُ بِعَمَلِ أَهْلِ الْجَنَّةِ حَتَّى مَا يَكُونُ بَيْنَهُ

وَبَيْنَهَا إِلَّا ذِرَاعٌ فَيَسْبِقُ عَلَيْهِ الكِتَابُ فَيَعْمَلُ بِعَمَلِ

أَهْلِ النَّارِ فَيَدْخُلُ النَّارَ

**"Indeed, a man does the deeds of the dwellers
of paradise until there is not between him and
it (i.e. paradise) but a hand span, then that
which has been written overtakes him, thus he
does the deeds of the inhabitants of the hell fire,
and enters it."**

Likewise it comes in some narrations of the hadith that
which explains and clarifies (this hadith). The Prophet
(May Allah raise his status and bestow upon him peace)
said:

إِنَّ الرَّجُلَ لَيَعْمَلُ بِعَمَلِ أَهْلِ الْجَنَّةِ فِيمَا يَبْدُو لِلنَّاسِ

**"Indeed, a man does the deeds of the dwellers
of paradise from that which is apparent to the
people."**

So due to this the scholars (may Allah have mercy upon
them) have taken (from this hadith) that the person
whose belief is correct, and is upright upon the religion
of Allah (Blessed and Exalted), then Allah will preserve
his religion, preserve his faith, and protect him –by this

favor and honor- from deviation and misguidance. And because of this Ibn Al-Qayyim (may Allah have mercy upon him) has reported in his book (Al-Jawaab Al-Kaafi) from one of the scholars that he stated:

"It is not perceived for the one whose belief was correct that the likes of this would happen to him (i.e. deviate), but rather the likes of this affair will only take place with regards to the person who was negligent, lacked concern, did not take heed or had with him deviation in the aspect of the belief. Due to this, the masters of innovation and the people of desires are from the people who are the greatest in deviating in the religion, changing from one way to another way, and from one path to another path. As for the correct belief and upright faith then it is a protection for its companion as well as a safety for him by the permission of Allah (Blessed and Exalted)."

PAYING ATTENTION TO THE CONDUCT OF THOSE WHO ARE GOOD EXAMPLES FROM THE SERVANTS OF ALLAH

Also from the means of staying firm upon the truth and guidance is paying attention to the conducts of those who are good examples from the servants of Allah, and the best of His servants; while contemplating their behavior, looking into their information, their character, their excellences, their great merit, and their bless morals. For indeed this is from the greatest aides in staying firm upon the truth and guidance. Specifically the conducts of the Prophets; the best of the servants of Allah, and they are the finest of His creation. Verily, within their stories are a lesson and example; and within them is an aide in staying steadfast and being upright upon the truth and guidance.

﴿وَكُلًّا نَقُصُّ عَلَيْكَ مِنْ أَنبَاءِ الرُّسُلِ مَا نُثَبِّتُ بِهِ فُؤَادَكَ﴾

"All that We relate to you from the news of the Messengers (is so that) We may make your heart firm thereby." [Hud 120]

Therefore, Allah's mention of the stories of the Prophets in the noble Quran is not just for information that we may know; or (just) stories and news that we are informed about. Rather, the intent of mentioning these stories is so that the believer may take thereby an example and benefit.

$$﴿لَقَدْ كَانَ فِي قَصَصِهِمْ عِبْرَةٌ لِّأُولِي الْأَلْبَابِ ۗ مَا كَانَ حَدِيثًا يُفْتَرَىٰ﴾$$

"Verily in their stories, is an example for those of understanding. It is not speech forged." [Yusuf 111]

Thus, their stories are an example and lesson for the believer. For this (reason) it is obligatory upon the diligent Muslim who is steadfast upon the truth and guidance to give great concern to the stories of the Prophets, and the news of the Messengers. Especially the news and biography of the best of them, and the finest of them; our Prophet Muhammad (May Allah raise his status and bestow upon him peace). Allah has said:

$$﴿لَقَدْ كَانَ لَكُمْ فِي رَسُولِ اللَّهِ أُسْوَةٌ حَسَنَةٌ لِّمَن كَانَ يَرْجُو اللَّهَ وَالْيَوْمَ الْآخِرَ وَذَكَرَ اللَّهَ كَثِيرًا ۝﴾$$

"You have in the Messenger of Allah the best example; for he who hopes for Allah and the

hereafter,and remembers Allah much. [Al-Ahzab 21]

So whenever the servant gives great concern to the biographies, and the news of the best of those individuals, then ones love will be greater for them. And whenever one has great love for them in their heart, then ones adherence to them will be greater, and one will transverse upon their way. Hence by that, one will be closer to good.

Look – May Allah protect you- at when many of the male and the female youth turned to reading the stories and the news of people who had no desire for good (nor were upright in the religion), how reading those stories of these people deceived the male and female youth; and how those stories became a reason for the deviation (of the youth), and kept them far away from the correct path. This clarifies to you that reading biographies whoever they may be, affects a person and that is a must. And it is not appropriate that a youth says: I just read biographies and news for entertainment and to past the time. However, this in reality is not the case. It is not just entertainment and passing the time, but rather in reality it has a negative (affect) upon (ones) faith and intellect. Likewise it pollutes the intellect and sickens it. Specifically those who are experts in the affair of stories, and deviating the minds; the minds of young and the youth; and (you could) say the same about the (T.V) series and plays, which many of the male and female youth have been tried with; and how with time these (things) have has a tremendous affect upon their faith, character, and manners.

For this reason it is imperative that a person is stern with them self; and that he does not read the biographies except the biographies of those who in reading their biography there is a benefit, and studying their news is useful and beneficial; from giving life to the hearts, renewing (ones) faith, correcting the belief, strengthening (ones) reliance, doing good deeds, and other than that. Just a person stated:

فَحَدِيثُهُمْ يَجْلُو الفُؤَادَ الصَّادِي   كَرِّرْ عَلَيَّ حَدِيثَهُمْ يَا حَادِي

"Repeat to me their speech O cameleer. Because their speech returns the vigor to the rusty heart."

Yes by Allah, this is the affair of the speech, the biographies, and the news of the righteous. It has a great affect upon the hearts. Due to this, it is a must that the Muslim who admonishes himself gives geart concern to reading the biographies of the Prophets, the news of the Messengers, and the biographies of those who followed the Prophets. The best of those who followed the Prophets are the noble companions (May Allah be pleased with them and they be pleased with Him)

﴿ كُنتُمْ خَيْرَ أُمَّةٍ أُخْرِجَتْ لِلنَّاسِ ﴾

"You were the best nation raised up for mankind." [Ali-Imran 110]

And because of this Allah (Exalted and Glorified) said:

﴿وَالسَّابِقُونَ الْأَوَّلُونَ مِنَ الْمُهَاجِرِينَ وَالْأَنْصَارِ
وَالَّذِينَ اتَّبَعُوهُم بِإِحْسَانٍ﴾

"The first and foremost of those who accepted Islam from the Muhajiroon and the Ansar; and those who followed them in goodness." [At-Tawbah 100]

A person will not truly follow them in goodness except if he knows them; he knows their news, he knows their biographies and circumstances, he strives against himself in following them, and traversing upon their upright way. Therefore, this affair is honorable and is of the uppermost importance. O you who has been granted success, when you read the biographies of the Prophets (May Allah raise their status and grant them peace) you find in every story that which aides you in strengthening (your) religion and making it firm, increasing you in certainty and putting reliance upon Allah (The Exalted). If you read about the patience of Nooh in calling and advising his people, and him working (diligently) to guide them, and that he remained a thousand years except fifty years; while calling his people night and day, secretly and publicly, with tremendous patience and utmost striving. By reading this it will have the greatest affect upon you.

If you read about the patience of Zakariya (May Allah grant him peace) during the calamity that Allah tested him with; and (how) he turned to Allah, seeking His protection, and relying upon him, then that will have the greatest affect upon you. And if you read the story of Yusuf (May Allah grant him peace), it's filled with examples and lessons. Ponder over his story with the wife of Al-Azeez and how she sought to seduce him, and she made that feasible for him. And she was (a women) of high status and beauty. So many temptations were present in that situation. Just a few of these (temptations) would have sufficed in displacing many people in a cesspit of vices. But despite the many different types of temptations Yusuf said:

"I seek refuge in Allah"

And he said as it comes in the whole story:

﴿رَبِّ السِّجْنُ أَحَبُّ إِلَيَّ مِمَّا يَدْعُونَنِي إِلَيْهِ﴾

"My Lord, prison is more beloved to me than that which they call me to."

Thus, when an individual reads the likes of these stories and this news. Especially the news of the last of the

Prophets; the finest of them and the best of them, our Prophet Muhammad (May Allah raise his status and bestow upon him peace), this has so much affect (upon a person). So for this reason the people are in need of reading the biography as well as reading the merits; the merits of the noble Prophet (May Allah raise his status and bestow upon him peace) so that this reading may be an aide for them –by Allah's permission- in staying steadfast upon the truth and guidance.

DILIGENCE IN CLOSING THOSE PATHWAYS THAT LEAD HIM TO DESTRUCTION

Also from the means of staying firm upon the truth and guidance is that a person is diligent in closing those pathways that lead him to destruction, and cause him to get involved in that which is unlawful. A person should not be negligent about this issue, but rather one is to strive against their self so that no inner thoughts may enter upon them from (ones) innermost feelings, which lead them to evil and corruption.

If you want to know the importance of this issue, then contemplate upon this affair in the tremendous hadith, which has been collected in the Musnad and other than it, that our noble Prophet (May Allah raise his status and bestow upon him peace) said:

ضَرَبَ اللَّهُ مَثَلًا صِرَاطًا مُسْتَقِيمًا، وَعَلَى جَنْبَتَيْ الصِّرَاطِ سُورَانِ فِيهِمَا أَبْوَابٌ مُفَتَّحَةٌ، وَعَلَى الْأَبْوَابِ سُتُورٌ مُرْخَاةٌ، وَعَلَى بَابِ الصِّرَاطِ دَاعٍ يَقُولُ أَيُّهَا النَّاسُ ادْخُلُوا الصِّرَاطَ جَمِيعًا وَلَا

تعوجوا، وَدَاعٍ يَدْعُو مِنْ جَوْفِ الصِّرَاطِ فَإِذَا أَرَادَ يَفْتَحُ شَيْئًا
مِنْ تِلْكَ الْأَبْوَابِ قَالَ وَيُحَكَ لَا تَفْتَحْهُ فَإِنَّكَ إِنْ تَفْتَحْهُ تَلِجْهُ
-ثم بين ذلك قال: - وَالصِّرَاطُ الْإِسْلَامُ، وَالسُّورَانِ حُدُودُ اللهِ
تَعَالَى، وَالْأَبْوَابُ الْمُفَتَّحَةُ مَحَارِمُ اللهِ تَعَالَى، وَذَلِكَ الدَّاعِي عَلَى
رَأْسِ الصِّرَاطِ كِتَابُ اللهِ عَزَّ وَجَلَّ، وَالدَّاعِي فَوْقَ الصِّرَاطِ
وَاعِظُ اللهِ فِي قَلْبِ كُلِّ مُسْلِمٍ

"Allah has made a parable of the straight path. On the two sides of the path are two walls with open doors. On each door there are curtains hanging, and at the door of the path is a caller saying: "O people, all of you enter the path (and be straight) and do not be crooked." And there will be a caller calling out from the inside of the path. So if one wants to open any of these doors (the caller) says to him: "Woe to you, do not open it. If you open it you will enter it."

Then he clarifies this saying:

"The path is Islam, and the two walls are the limits set by Allah. And the open doors are what Allah has forbidden. The caller at the head of the path is the book of Allah, and the caller above the path is the admonisher of Allah, which is in the heart of every Muslim."

So here we contemplate - O traveler- as you walk along the straight path- that it does not cease (as long as) you are on your path - doors passing your right and your left leading a person to enter into that which is unlawful, and deviating (a person) from the straight path. These doors are described in this hadith as having curtains hanging upon them. And you know that a door that does not have anything on it except a curtain, that the one entering it does not require much effort, nor does it require from him (a lot) of time. Contrary to the door that has a lock on it, and needs handling and effort; and opening it requires time from a person. As for those doors that lead a person to the unlawful, which only have curtains on them; and curtains do not require from a person much effort in opening them. So if the traveler stops in his path and just says: I'm going to look, just a glance." Then after the glance is a gradually step, then after that step he sets out until a person finds himself involved (in haram).

For this reason it is a must that the diligent person upon steadfastness and uprightness upon the truth and guidance, to close (all of) the pathways, and that he does not open anything from them, least he be destroyed. Many people have become involved (in the haram). Especially in this time, with the new devices like the cell phones, which are carried and transported. A person transports it with him from place to place. Likewise the devices in homes and what they contain from many sites, which are infested with desires, and doubts. Many people due to (their) lack of deen, weakness of faith, and feeble knowledge, many of them do not care, and say:"

I'm just getting on the site and looking." "What do they have, and what do they have".

Then he finds himself with time, and because of this looking and listening, he finds that inner thoughts have started to enter his heart, and many things have accumulated upon his heart, because of looking and listening. And he is the one who has perpetrated this against himself. He was thinking in the beginning that he would enter (upon these sites), and would not be affected. However, within days he finds that this really has caused his heart to become tremendously sick. So his situation was like that of the one who said:

$$أَلْقَاهُ فِي الْيَمِ مَكْتُوفًا وَقَالَ لَهُ ۚ إِيَّاكَ إِيَّاكَ أَنْ تبتل بِالْمَاءِ$$

"It casted him in the sea tied up, and said to him: Beware! Beware! Least that you become wet with water!"

So how can a person hope for themselves safety and well-being and he has plunged and put himself on a path that results in one's destruction and leads to ruin. If you want to know an example that will bring you closer to (understanding) this illustration; and the scholars have mentioned it – Imam Ahmad and other than him- regarding the circumstance of the servant. How when he first falls into sins, he falls into very minor things. Then he does not cease to delve and drift until he is contaminated with dangerous great types of sins. The scholars have mentioned an example of that: Have you seen a person who has on clean clothes with new clean shoes? He passes through an area that has mud and clay in it; and he is in need of passing this area. What does he do in the beginning of the affair? You find that he searches for a tall rock, or an elevated place, which does not have mud or clay on it. Thus, he places his foot on it while being extremely cautious. He walks in the mud while putting his foot on things that haven't been touched by the mud and clay, then he continues. Sometimes, perhaps he slips and gets hit with a little (mud). But he does not cease being diligent, so that he does not touch anything from this mud. Then he slips (again), then a second time, then a third. Then he dives into it and doesn't even care.

This is an example that the scholars have illustrated to show how things start with a person little by little, until a great involvement in sins take place, as well as delving into them. Because of this, from the greatest affairs and the most important of them with regards to staying firm upon the truth and guidance, is that a person closes (all those) pathways, which result in him falling into the unlawful; and that he does not following the footsteps of shaytan.

A PERSON IS EXTREMELY DILIGENT ABOUT FRIENDS AND COMPANIONS

Also from the ways of staying steadfast upon the truth and guidance, is that a person is extremely diligent about friends and companions. And that one chooses for himself companions and friends who will assist him upon steadfastness. Because the companion trails along and affects his companion, and that is unavoidable. Due to this the Prophet (May Allah raise his status and bestow upon him peace) said:

الْمَرْءُ عَلَى دِينِ خَلِيلِهِ فَلْيَنْظُرْ أَحَدُكُمْ مَنْ يُخَالِلُ

"A person is on the religion of his friend, so let one of you look to whom he takes as a friend."

Likewise he (May Allah raise his status and bestow upon him peace) said:

مَثَلُ الْجَلِيسِ الصَّالِحِ وَالْجَلِيسِ السَّوْءِ كَحَامِلِ الْمِسْكِ وَنَافِخِ
الْكِيرِ؛ فَحَامِلُ الْمِسْكِ إِمَّا أَنْ يُحْذِيَكَ، وَإِمَّا أَنْ تَبْتَاعَ مِنْهُ،
وَإِمَّا أَنْ تَجِدَ مِنْهُ رِيحًا طَيِّبَةً، وَنَافِخُ الْكِيرِ إِمَّا أَنْ يُحْرِقَ ثِيَابَكَ،
وَإِمَّا أَنْ تَجِدَ رِيحًا خَبِيثَةً

"The example of the righteous companion whom is sat with, and the bad companion whom is sat with, is like that of the one carrying musk, and the blacksmith blowing bellows. As for the one carrying musk then either he will give you some as a gift, or you will buy some from him, or you will find a nice smell from him. As for the blacksmith blowing bellows, he will either burn your clothes or you will find a foul smell from him."

For this reason, in this situation the servant is in need of choosing companions who will assist him in obedience (to Allah), strengthen his ability, and strengthen his arm in the obedience of Allah. Allah (Exalted and Majestic) said:

$$﴾سَنَشُدُّ عَضُدَكَ بِأَخِيكَ﴿$$

"We will strengthen your arm thorough your brother." [Al-Qasas 35]

Also Allah said:

$$﴾وَاصْبِرْ نَفْسَكَ مَعَ الَّذِينَ يَدْعُونَ رَبَّهُم بِالْغَدَاةِ وَالْعَشِيِّ يُرِيدُونَ وَجْهَهُ ۖ وَلَا تَعْدُ عَيْنَاكَ عَنْهُمْ تُرِيدُ زِينَةَ الْحَيَاةِ الدُّنْيَا ۖ وَلَا تُطِعْ مَنْ أَغْفَلْنَا قَلْبَهُ عَن ذِكْرِنَا وَاتَّبَعَ هَوَاهُ وَكَانَ أَمْرُهُ فُرُطًا ۝﴿$$

"Be patient with those who call upon their Lord during the early morning and in the evening desiring His face. And do not let your eyes over look them, desiring the glitter of the life of this world. And do not obey he whom We have made his heart heedless of Our remembrance; and follows his desire, and whose deed has been made lost." [Al-Kahf 28]

This situation – the situation of choosing companions- is a situation that requires understanding and contemplation with regards to the one a person takes as a companion. It is not for the believer to go with whoever he wants. Rather, he is to choose brothers, companions, and friends who will aide him in good. This is what is benefited from the statement of our Prophet (May Allah raise his status and bestow upon him peace) in the previous hadith,

فَلْيَنْظُرْ أَحَدُكُمْ مَنْ يُخَالِلْ

"So let one of you look to whom he takes as a friend."

His statement: "So let one look to", this is a request from our Prophet (May Allah raise his status and bestow upon him peace) to have understanding in this affair, and to contemplate it. So a person contemplates and looks to the one who he is going to accompany and associate with, then after that he befriends them. Due to this some of the salaf stated:

مِنْ فِقْهِ الرَّجُلِ مَدْخُلُهُ وَمَخْرَجُهُ وَأُلْفُهُ مِنَ النَّاسِ

"From the understanding of a man is who he enters with, who he leaves with, and who he befriends from the people."

This is a proof for having understanding. And due to this it is appropriate that a person gives great concern to choosing noble companions, and brothers who will aide him in knowledge, aide him in being prepared, aide him in righteousness and adherence to the obedience of Allah (Blessed and Exalted).

THE MUSLIM KNOWS THAT HE HAS AN ENEMY WHO DOES NOT WANT HIM TO BE FIRM

Also from the ways of staying firm is that the Muslim knows that he has an enemy who does not want him to be firm, nor does he want him to be upright upon the obedience of Allah (Glorified and Exalted). And from the affair of this enemy is that he sees you, and you do not see him. An enemy who sees you, but you do not see (him) is a strong ammunition, as the salaf (may Allah have mercy upon them) have stated. This enemy, Allah has ordered us to take him as an enemy, and He (Glorified and Exalted) warned us from (following) his footsteps, his evil, and his deception.

$$﴿إِنَّ الشَّيْطَانَ لَكُمْ عَدُوٌّ فَاتَّخِذُوهُ عَدُوًّا إِنَّمَا يَدْعُو حِزْبَهُ لِيَكُونُوا مِنْ أَصْحَابِ السَّعِيرِ ۝﴾$$

"Indeed, shaytan is an enemy to you, so take him as an enemy. He only invites his party (i.e. followers) so that they may be from dwellers of the blazing fire" [Fatir 6]

﴿ يَا أَيُّهَا الَّذِينَ آمَنُوا لَا تَتَّبِعُوا خُطُوَاتِ الشَّيْطَانِ ﴾

**"O you who believe, do not follow the footsteps
of shaytan."** [An-Noor 21]

And due to this it is imperative that a person pays close
attention to the dangers of this enemy. And that this
enemy does not cease to be with the servant (of Allah)
misguiding, preventing, and sitting in the servants path
ways.

﴿ ثُمَّ لَآتِيَنَّهُم مِّن بَيْنِ أَيْدِيهِمْ وَمِنْ خَلْفِهِمْ وَعَنْ أَيْمَانِهِمْ
وَعَن شَمَائِلِهِمْ ۖ وَلَا تَجِدُ أَكْثَرَهُمْ شَاكِرِينَ ﴿١٧﴾ ﴾

**"Then I will come to them in front of them and
behind them, from their right and their left, and
You (i.e. Allah) will not find most of them
thankful."** [Al-Araf 17]

The Prophet (May Allah raise his status and bestow upon
him peace) said:

إِنَّ الشَّيْطَانَ قَعَدَ لِابْنِ آدَمَ بِأَطْرُقِهِ

**"Verily, shaytan sits in the path ways of the son
of Adam."**

Meaning every path that the servant pursues, whether it
be a good path or an evil path. Shaytan even sits in his
path of good; in order to divert him and turn him away,

as well as to weaken the servants worship and him seeking nearness to Allah. For this reason, it is legislated for us – when we enter that masjid- to say:

أَعُوذُ بِاللَّهِ الْعَظِيمِ وَبِوَجْهِهِ الْكَرِيمِ وَسُلْطَانِهِ الْقَدِيمِ مِنَ الشَّيْطَانِ الرَّجِيمِ

"I seek refuge in Allah the Magnificent, and in His noble Face, and in His eternal Sovereignty from the accursed shaytan. "

Also it is legislated for us when we leave the masjid to say:

اللَّهُمَّ أَعِذْنَا مِنَ الشَّيْطَانِ

"O Allah, protect us from shaytan."

Because shaytan sits for the son of Adam in every path that the servant pursues, and every road that the servant walks through, be it good or evil. If the path is good, it is so that shaytan can turn him way, and if it is that of evil then shaytan pushes him to proceed and continue there in. So due to this, it is a must that the diligent servant upon steadfastness and uprightness, who is safe from deviation and misguidance to know the dangers of this enemy; and he should increase in seeking refuge in Allah from him.

﴿وَقُل رَّبِّ أَعُوذُ بِكَ مِنْ هَمَزَاتِ الشَّيَاطِينِ ۝ وَأَعُوذُ
بِكَ رَبِّ أَن يَحْضُرُونِ ۝﴾

"And say: My Lord, I seek refuge in you from the whispers of the devils. And I seek refuge in you My Lord that they should come near me." [Al-Muminoon 97-98]

﴿قُلْ أَعُوذُ بِرَبِّ النَّاسِ ۝ مَلِكِ النَّاسِ ۝ إِلَهِ النَّاسِ ۝ مِن شَرِّ الْوَسْوَاسِ الْخَنَّاسِ ۝ الَّذِى يُوَسْوِسُ فِى صُدُورِ النَّاسِ ۝ مِنَ الْجِنَّةِ وَالنَّاسِ ۝﴾

"Say: I seek refuge in the Lord of mankind. The King of mankind. The God of Mankind. From the evil of the whispers of the one who withdraws. Who whispers into the breast of mankind. Of Jinn and men." [An-Naas 1-6]

Therefore, he withdraws from whispering. If the servant is negligent of the remembrance of Allah then he whispers, but if the servant remembers Allah he withdraws. Meaning he leaves the servant. Allah said:

﴿وَمَن يَعْشُ عَن ذِكْرِ الرَّحْمَنِ نُقَيِّضْ لَهُ شَيْطَانًا فَهُوَ لَهُ قَرِينٌ ۝﴾

"And whosoever turns away from the remembrance of the Most Merciful, then We will appoint to him a devil companion." [Az-Zukruf 36]

THE SERVANT ALWAYS REMEMBERS THAT THIS LIFE IS A PLACE FOR PASSING THROUGH

Also from the ways that aide in steadfastness is that the servant always remember that this life is (just) a place for passing through, and not a place for settlement. One should remind themselves of the standing before Allah, and His meeting. And that Allah will reward the servants, and that their accounting is based upon their deeds. Alee ibn Abee Taalib (May Allah be pleased with him) stated:

ارْتَحَلَتِ الدُّنْيَا مُدْبِرَةً، وَارْتَحَلَتِ الآخِرَةُ مُقْبِلَةً، وَلِكُلِّ وَاحِدَةٍ مِنْهُمَا بَنُونَ، فَكُونُوا مِنْ أَبْنَاءِ الآخِرَةِ وَلاَ تَكُونُوا مِنْ أَبْنَاءِ الدُّنْيَا ، فَإِنَّ اليَوْمَ عَمَلٌ وَلاَ حِسَابَ، وَغَدًا حِسَابٌ وَلاَ عَمَلٌ

"Verily, the worldly life is departing, and the hereafter is coming; and they both have children. Therefore, be from the children of the hereafter, and do not be from the children of this worldly life. For indeed today is action with no account, and tomorrow is account with no action."

So due this, from the greatest matters which aide in steadfastness and guidance, is that the servant constantly remembers that he will stand before Allah. And that he will meet Allah, and that there will be an account, punishment, paradise, hell-fire, pleasure, and displeasure; he remembers this. Indeed, remembering this and reflecting about it is from the greatest affairs which aide one upon the truth and guidance. For this reason the person who is given their book (i.e. record of deeds) in their right hand, and returns towards his family joyed and happy of (his) book; what does he mention for the reason of his safety and success?

﴿فَأَمَّا مَنْ أُوتِيَ كِتَابَهُ بِيَمِينِهِ فَيَقُولُ هَاؤُمُ اقْرَءُوا كِتَابِيَهْ ۝ إِنِّي ظَنَنتُ أَنِّي مُلَاقٍ حِسَابِيَهْ ۝﴾

"As for the he who is given his book in his right hand he will say: Here! Read my book! I knew I would meet my account! [Al-Haaqah 19-20]

This is the reason. "I knew", meaning: I believed I would meet my account. This belief if it clings to the heart and is grounded in the soul, and the servant reflects about it, then it will be an aide for him – by Allah's permission- upon steadfastness on the truth and guidance. Similar to this is Allah's saying:

﴿إِنَّا كُنَّا قَبْلُ فِي أَهْلِنَا مُشْفِقِينَ ۝ فَمَنَّ اللَّهُ عَلَيْنَا وَوَقَانَا عَذَابَ السَّمُومِ ۝﴾

"Verily, before we were afraid amongst our families. So Allah has been favored us and has saved us from the torment of the fire." [At-Toor 26-27]

Therefore, the likes of this contemplating and reflecting will aid the servant upon steadfastness, the truth, and guidance. Due to this Allah says:

$$﴿ يَا أَيُّهَا الَّذِينَ آمَنُوا اتَّقُوا اللَّهَ وَلْتَنظُرْ نَفْسٌ مَّا قَدَّمَتْ لِغَدٍ ۖ وَاتَّقُوا اللَّهَ ﴾$$

"O you who have believed, fear Allah, and let every soul look to what It has put forth for tomorrow. And fear Allah..." [Al-Hashr 18]

So this consideration – a person's consideration- for what his soul has put forth for tomorrow, what has he done? What is he going to meet Allah with? He should look and take account of himself. Take account of yourselves before you are taken into account. And weight your actions before they are presented before Allah (Blessed and Exalted). So the likes of this consideration, contemplation, and constantly reflecting about this is from the greatest aid for staying frim upon the truth and guidance. For this reason you find in many Ahadeeth (i.e. plural of hadith) in the context of mentioning righteous deeds, or the context of warning against wicked actions. The Prophet (May Allah raise his status and bestow upon him peace) said:

مَنْ كَانَ يُؤْمِنُ بِاللَّهِ وَالْيَوْمِ الآخِرِ

"Whoever believes in Allah and the last day."

This is because remembering the last day, which is the day of recompense and the day of account, will strengthen within the servant the devotion for acts of obedience, and keep him away from sin and the unlawful. Allah (Glorified and Exalted) said:

﴿وَتَزَوَّدُوا فَإِنَّ خَيْرَ الزَّادِ التَّقْوَىٰ ۚ وَاتَّقُونِ يَا أُولِي الْأَلْبَابِ ۝﴾

"So take a provision, for indeed the best provision is piety. And fear Me, O men of understanding." [Al-Baqarah 197]

TAKING ONE'S SELF INTO ACCOUNT

Also from the important ways that assist in steadfastness is taking one's self into account. And that a person looks to his deeds and what he has put forth. And that his taking account of himself is greater than that of a (business) partner taking account of his partner. He takes account of himself. It's better for him to take account of himself (now) before Allah takes him into account. Because if he takes account of himself he will look to his deeds, and he will realize his negligence and his shortcomings. This is from the reasons for leaving off this negligence, and staying away from carelessness and being undutiful to Allah. So it is better for the servant that he takes account of himself before he says –and it will not benefit him to say this-

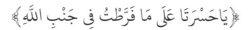

"Atlas, my grief that I was undutiful to Allah."
[Az-Zumar 56]

This is a tremendous situation that is evitable. And the verse that has already been mentioned, and it is Allah's saying:

﴿يَا أَيُّهَا الَّذِينَ آمَنُوا اتَّقُوا اللَّهَ وَلْتَنظُرْ نَفْسٌ مَّا قَدَّمَتْ لِغَدٍ ۖ وَاتَّقُوا اللَّهَ ۚ إِنَّ اللَّهَ خَبِيرٌ بِمَا تَعْمَلُونَ ﴿١٨﴾﴾

"O you who have believed, fear Allah, and let every soul look to what it has put forth for tomorrow, and fear Allah. Indeed Allah Knows well that which you do." [Al-Hashr 18]

(This verse) is a foundation in this affair, the affair of takings one's self into account.

CLOSING

So in closing, the ways and the methods that aide in firmness are many and various. It is obligatory that the servant contemplates well about this tremendous matter; especially that which relates to the hearts. This also is an important affair as it relates to staying firm upon the truth and guidance; that a person is diligent about the integrity of their heart and its soundness. The Prophet (May Allah raise his status and bestow upon him peace) said:

أَلاَ وَإِنَّ فِي الجَسَدِ مُضْغَةً إِذَا صَلَحَتْ صَلَحَ الجَسَدُ كُلُّهُ، وَإِذَا فَسَدَتْ فَسَدَ الجَسَدُ كُلُّهُ؛ أَلاَ وَهِيَ القَلْبُ

"Verily, in the body is a morsel of flesh. If it is upright then the whole body will be upright. But if it is corrupt then the entire body will be corrupt; indeed it is the heart."

Due to this, it is imperative that the servant is diligent about the uprightness of his heart, the soundness of his heart, and the purity of his inner self. Indeed the heart, if it is sound and upright, the body will be upright, because the body follows the heart as it relates to uprightness. The body follows the heart, and also the tongue. Due to this it was said:

الْمَرْءُ بِأَصْغَرَيْهِ

"The human personality is one of two things"

Meaning his heart and his tongue. The Prophet (May Allah raise his status and bestow upon him peace) said:

إِذَا أَصْبَحَ ابْنُ آدَمَ فَإِنَّ الأَعْضَاءَ كُلَّهَا تُكَفِّرُ اللِّسَانَ فَتَقُولُ: اتَّقِ اللَّهَ فِينَا فَإِنَّمَا نَحْنُ بِكَ، فَإِنِ اسْتَقَمْتَ اسْتَقَمْنَا ، وَإِنِ اعْوَجَجْتَ اعْوَجَجْنَا

"When the son of Adam wakes up, all of the limbs humble themselves before the tongue, and say: Fear Allah for our sake because we are with you. If you are upright we will be upright, but if you are crooked then we will be crooked."

Thus, if the servant is granted success with a sound heart and upright tongue all his deeds will be sound. Likewise from the great supplications in this affair, and it is a bless supplication that has been established from our noble Prophet (May Allah raise his status and bestow upon him peace) and it is in Mujam At-Tabarani, and other than it, from the hadith of Shaddad ibn Aws (May Allah be pleased with him) that the Prophet (May Allah raise his status and bestow upon him peace) said to him:

إِذَا رَأَيْتَ النَّاسَ قَدِ اكْتَنَزُوا الذَّهَبَ وَالْفِضَّةَ فَاكْنِزْ هَؤُلَاءِ الْكَلِمَاتِ: اللَّهُمَّ إِنِّي أَسْأَلُكَ الثَّبَاتَ فِي الأَمْرِ وَالْعَزِيمَةَ عَلَى

الرُّشْدِ، وَأَسْأَلُكَ مُوجِبَاتِ رَحْمَتِكَ وَعَزَائِمَ مَغْفِرَتِكَ، وَأَسْأَلُكَ
شُكْرَ نِعْمَتِكَ وَحُسْنَ عِبَادَتِكَ ، وَأَسْأَلُكَ قَلْبًا سَلِيمًا وَلِسَانًا
صَادِقًا ، وَأَسْأَلُكَ مِنْ خَيْرِ مَا تَعْلَمُ، وَأَعُوذُ بِكَ مِنْ شَرِّ مَا تَعْلَمُ،
وَأَسْتَغْفِرُكَ لِمَا تَعْلَمُ ، إِنَّكَ أَنْتَ عَلامُ الْغُيُوبِ

"If you see the people have gathered gold and silver, then gather these words: O Allah, I ask you for steadfastness in (my) affair and determination in (following) the right path. I ask You for that which necessitates Your mercy, and the decision of Your forgiveness. I ask You to make me thankful of Your blessings, and to worship you properly. I ask You for a sound heart and truthful tongue. I ask You for the good of what You know, and I seek refuge in You from the evil of what You know, verily, You know the unseen."

In closing I ask Allah the Generous, Lord of the great throne, by His beautiful names and His lofty attributes, that He benefit everyone with that which He has taught us, and to increase us in knowledge. And that he rectifies for us all of our affairs, and that He does not leave us to ourselves for the blinking of an eye. O Allah, guide all of us to You upon the straight path. O Changer of hearts, make our hearts firm upon Your religion. Our Lord, do not deviate our hearts after You have guided us, and grant us mercy from You, indeed You are the Giver. O Allah, we seek refuge with you that we misguide or that we are misguided, that we fall into error or that we are made to fall into error, that we oppress or that we are oppressed, that we behave ignorantly or we are treated in an ignorant manner. O Allah, give our souls their piety and purify them, You are the best who purifies them, You are their Guardian and Protector. O Allah, we ask you for guidance, piety, chastity, and self- sufficiency. O Allah, we ask you for guidance and uprightness. O Allah, to You we submit, in You we believe, in You we put our trust, to You we turn in repentance and with Your help we contend our adversaries. We seek refuge in You that You misguide us, You are the All- Living who never dies, but jinn and mankind will all die. O Allah, we ask you for all good now and latter, that which we know of it and that which we do not know. We seek refuge with You from all evil now and latter, that which we know of it and that which we do not know. O Allah, we ask You for paradise and that which will bring (us) near it from statement and action, and we seek refuge with You from the hell-fire and that which will bring (us) near it from statement and action. O Allah, we ask You for the good that Your servant and messenger Muhammad (May Allah raise his status and bestow upon him peace) asked You for, and we seek refuge with You from the evil that Your servant and messenger Muhammad (May Allah raise his status and bestow upon him peace) sought refuge in You from; and that You make all our ordainment that You have ordain for us good. O Allah, protect us and (all) the Muslims wherever they may be from trials, that which is apparent from it and that which is hidden. O, Allah we seek refuge in You from tribulations, that which is apparent from it and that which is hidden. O Allah, we seek refuge in You from tribulations, that which is apparent from it and that which is hidden. O Allah, grant us security in our countries and rectify our leaders and rulers, and make our leadership with he who fears You, is devote to You, and follows what you are pleased with, O Lord of the worlds. Our Lord, we have wronged ourselves and if You do not forgive us and have mercy upon us, we will surely be from the losers. Our Lord, give us good in this life and good in the hereafter, and save us from the punishment of the fire. O Allah, fogive us, our parents, our scholars, or rulers, the Muslims male and female, the believers male and female, those who are alive from them and the deceased. O Allah, apportion for us fear that serves as a barrier between us and acts of disobedience; and obedience that will take us to Your paradise; and certainty that will make it easy for us to bear the calamities of this world. O Allah, allow us to enjoy our hearing, our sight and our strength as long as You keep us alive, and make it the inheritor of us, and make our revenge for those who oppress us, and aide us against those who are hostile towards us, and do not make our calamity in our religion, nor make this world our greatest concern, nor the limit of our knowledge, nor give power over us to those who will not have mercy upon us. Glorified are You O Allah, praise be to You. I testify that there is not deity worthy of worship but You. I seek Your pardon and turn to You in repentance. O Allah, raise the status and grant peace to Your servant and messenger, our Prophet Muhammad, his family and his companions.

Made in the USA
Middletown, DE
20 June 2024